Life and Love:

Musings from a Poet's Heart

Lisa Boyd

Copyright © 2020 Lisa Boyd

All rights reserved. No part of this book may be copied, reproduced, redistributed nor transmitted in any way without the express written consent and approval of the author.

ISBN: 978-0-578-64255-0

DEDICATION

This is dedicated to Whitelow and Lannie Boyd of Fayette County in Oakland, Tennessee.

ACKNOWLEDGMENTS

Whitelow and Lannie Boyd—I never forget my grassroots and where I came from. My grandparents were farmers; they adopted us and raised me in the country. I remember picking and chopping cotton in the fields. They grew fruits and vegetables and raised livestock; this provided food for the family. Looking back, those were the good old days and some of the best days of my life. I was so happy playing by myself as a child. I looked up to them as being the best parents in the world.

Thanks to Ann Boyd, LaShonda Boyd, and my son Denzel Bowman for their love and support.

Thanks to my FedEx family.

Sometimes you don't have to be beautiful outside... because you're already beautiful just being you!

Lisa Boyd

RUNNING

I Feel like running,
I see my shoes, but I can't find my feet.
I feel like running,
But I'm unable, all I seem to do is sleep.
I feel like running,
But I'm like a boat without a sail,
I feel like running,
Like a poor woman that just got a million dollars in the mail,
I feel like running,
All I need are some wings,
I feel like running,
Maybe just maybe I could make it to Heaven and hear God's angels sing,
I feel like running,
Although my spirits are low,
I feel like running,
Although there may be no place to go,
I feel like running,
It just may ease my burdens and pains,
I feel like running,
To rid myself of invisible chains,
Someday I'll stop running,
I'll face myself, deal with me,
I'll be ecstatic and joyful,
About the person I see.

PERFECT WORLD

I see perfect people, in this perfect world, women must
have perfect hair, perfect strands, and perfect curls,
Yes, even perfect skin and perfect teeth, perfect outfits
and shoes on their feet,
Men must have the perfect girl, perfect cars, perfect
hair cut, and their mustaches groomed to perfection,
Somehow to me these things have become an
obsession,
I am however, totally the opposite, I make mistakes, I
don't talk proper, I don't walk straight, work, or live in
perfection,
My thoughts will stray, I will be driving, and turn the
wrong way,
I make mistakes and make excuses for them, then I'll
say, well it's all good, it's perfectly okay,
I need glasses to help me see, I talk too low and slow
where people can't hear me,
My hair gets messy and out of whack,
I can only touch it up and fix it back,
I'm not a perfect parent, I could always do better,
It's so hard to do everything right, but the most
important thing to me is that we love each other,
I can't be perfect, I don't know how,
Strive as I may,
Someone will always have something negative to say,
Leave me alone and leave me be!
Because, I have a perfectly good heart working inside
of me.

A WINTER'S POEM

Winter brings snow and ice, and playful snowball fights,
Christmas gifts and a solace life, and a time of the birth of Jesus Christ,
It's cold and freezing that never gets old,
Moma and Daddy making fires by our rustic stove,
Snuggling up to
A warm cozy fire,
Making a Christmas list with all my desire,
This being the coldest season of the year,
With Christmas fast approaching which I hold so dear,
Some may love the cold, crisp, dry air,
With people dressed like Eskimos that make you stop and stare,
Try to succumb through the cold winter months to come, December, January, and February alike,
Slipping and sliding; just fell down on some ice yikes, oh yikes,
We surrender our fun outside for activities to the inside for a little while,
Such a big adjustment for the walkers, joggers, and athlete's style,
There is a splendor in its presence, I respect the snow,
Where and when it comes from surely only my God knows,
It gives you shivers, and freezes the rivers,
In the winter months; word to the wise,
Don't stay outside, come in and thaw!
You can find this all written in the Winter Book of Winter's Law.

MY LITTLE DOVE

Hello my little dove,
Where are you headed? For Heaven up above,
Hello my little sister,
Yes, one is a pretty white and one is a beautiful black.
But when one dove stumbles and falls the other one picks up the slack,
We are a pair we will never separate,
Only until God comes and opens its pearly gates,
I've known you for almost an eternity,
And have enjoyed the blissful journey,
I know your heart and you know mine,
Look at us looking like one of a kind,
My heart will love you forever and a day,
And our friendship will last forever, and will never go away.

MY BABY

My baby is so beautiful, sweet, and carefree,
He bites, plays, and hits, yet, I know he loves,
He's a blessing from God and I thank Him every day,
As all children are made differently even odd in their own way,
As he sleeps I watch him breathe, in and out,
Thinking he's a little angel without a doubt,
Precious is he I love him so,
The greatest love of all he can take with him wherever he goes,
He is mine for now; some day to be a man,
The time is now I train and teach him the best I can,
He will make his own choices when he is grown,
But if he ever needs his moma,
He knows he can always call home.

THE GRADUATE

It seems as though, not long ago you were just a
little girl I used to play with,
In your lifetime you will encounter many things,
Remember this,
Learn to put your problems at the bottom of your
feet and God at the head of your life,
Problems are inevitable, but with God on your side
anything is possible,
This is the beginning of a wonderful life,
It's up to you in what you make of it and out of it,
To make your dreams all come true pray it, believe
it, and you will surely one day
Achieve it.

MY FLOWER

I know my flowers are so beautiful, and doesn't last for long,
Even though I love them and nurture them to grow beautifully strong,
Although you're so far away, can you hear me?
Can you hear my heart talking,
Can you feel it, can you feel that cloud where my mind is walking,
It's so loud, it's so clear you would think that I'm oh so near,
Yes, you light my fire, and filled me with such burning desire,
Ask me what is sweet and I'd say it is you as a treat,
Ask me what is making love to you and I'd say it's my dream come true,
Ask me what is sunny and bright, it's being with you, you're a sheer delight,
Ask me where a smile comes from, out of nowhere,
Sure I'd say, just knowing you and how much I care,
Mistakenly, you're the rose that stood afar,
Or could it be you're that twinkling, beaming, shining star,
So my Flower, please know, I carry you with me every day and every hour.

MY KNIGHT AND SHINING ARMOR

Hello beautiful, sexy, how was your day,
These are the words you'd always say,
I had become dark, gray, oblivious to feeling,
Your words became my source of power, and ultimate healing,
Just when I thought I would never love again,
You gently knocked at my door and said try me… Let me in!
You brought me laughter and joy even after,
A breath of fresh air no one could capture,
You have a savvy, swagger, way you walk,
And a cool calm convincing way when you talk,
You're a man of amazement and sweet allure,
A man forever in my heart that is totally pure,
When I'm in need you come to my distress like an angel watching over me,
I'm truly blessed:
Sometimes I get weak and about to falter,
Somehow you'd always appear like my knight in shining Armor,
Me the princess and damsel in distress,
Has found her prince at last,
It's you that stood out from all the rest,
So proud and valiantly,
You passed the test.

LOVE THAT CHANGED LIKE THE SEASONS

Like the leaves change as Autumn appears,
Our love so changed, but only now it's clear,
Somehow, I knew we'd soon depart,
And there I would lay with a shattered heart,
Though my eyes stayed closed to the actual fact,
Inside I knew I couldn't get you back,
What season did we alternate?
What decision did you make?
We withered like the golden brown leaves,
But somehow knew we'd never achieve,
Love was crushed like a child tramples on the leaves as if they'd never once lived,
So, as our love did because of the love you wouldn't give,
Questions are asked what went wrong,
We had a true love that made a bond so strong,
Our love was like a brisk cool breeze of summer air,
That came at that unbearable hot moment you asked God for it,
A wise statement to brand on yourself,
Learn life quickly so you won't be left,
So, deep and dearly my love flowed for you,
So, I'll pray for a blessing to your whole life through,
I'll miss the happy times that we shared together,
But, I wish you well in all your endeavors.

EXPRESSIONS OF MY LOVE

Sometimes it's hard to express myself,
This love I feel for no one else,
I knew I needed someone that cared,
And out of nowhere you were there,
I'll try to muscle my courage and say those things I've
locked in storage far away,
I prayed to God for a love that's true,
And by His grace He sent me to you,
There were times I doubted our affair,
But soon we became the perfect pair,
Let's try to keep our love flowing,
And keep that love fire going,
My life without you would be lonely and dull,
So, take this to heart, you are my true love.

OUR LOVE LIFE STORY

So, many years and memories have passed us by,
Filled with laughter, pain and bittersweet days that sometimes made me cry,
Never knowing the outcome from the very start,
Just following the instincts of true love that impaled my heart,
Love from you overwhelmed my life,
From this derived visions to be your wife,
When you held me so tight you said I could stay there,
Forever,
So, you held on and promised to me you would leave me
Never.

SILENT CRUSH

It was dangerously real my silent crush,
Your mind and thoughts became so surreal,
Conversations to my pretend lover,
All about the joy and pleasure he will discover,
Now you've found he doesn't share your heart,
Oh, so sad and devastating it has torn you apart,
I thought I'd write of how I love you so,
Instead I carry tears in my eyes, because you pushed me away,
Crushing all my dreams to lay in your arms every day,
I know you don't love me,
And will never take me as your bride,
So, I must relinquish my heart and pick up my pride.

NO MAN

I Ain't got no man,
Now ain't that a shame,
No kissing, no hugging,
Laying in my bed can't get no loving,
Here's five here's ten,
Lord I'll pay for it then,
See my sweat is steadily popping,
Looking out my window hoping a man will come along hopping,
Feeling so damn kinky,
You know where you get funky, stinky,
My nature is self-rising,
Couldn't get no hotter or I'd need to be put out with a fire hydrant,
I'll take one kinky, ugly, blue, or black,
The kind that would make you throw his ugly butt back,
Desperate, I say, No Man…..
Oh well, for me that's everyday

LOVE HAS BLOSSOMED

Listen to my heart, it has sounds of love ringing,
Look into my eyes, they speak the truth and carry in-depth meaning,
Take my hand and feel the warmth of love that grasps you, never letting go,
Take my word, it carries vows of promises guaranteed,
As the sun in its radiant glow,
Here and now I am open and vulnerable to love,
Here and readily now I am open, steadfast to love and to all acceptance of love,
I have surrendered my sword and shield of armor,
Never to sleep my life, never to slumber,
I pray to God, where all our help lies,
Never has there been a love so true,
I know it will continue in paradise, just laid away,
I'll take the joy and pain it brings and always treasure the sweet little things.

I LOVED YOU WHEN

I loved you when I first heard your voice, and then our love just took its course,
I loved you when I saw your face, a boyish look that filled the place,
I loved every minute we spent together,
Planning our love to last forever,
You were the one that made this life worth living,
All the love that you were giving,
It came to be a love of the past,
All we had just wouldn't last,
I thought it was over, I thought love was gone,
But you called and said you were coming home,
You were so sweet and good to me,
You made my dreams a reality
Blind to your line I said yes,
But it turned out to be just a joke I guess,
I loved you when?
Through it all and I'll love you Spring, Summer, Winter and Fall.

THIS I KNOW

Without saying a word, your acts of kindness were being observed
This I know
The clothes on your family's back are another example of your unselfish acts,
This I know
There is food in your house one way or another,
Determined that your children will be fed first one to the other,
This I know
And how do I know for I dwell not in your home,
Simply because your good works stand out proudly, all you've done alone, all you've done just on your own,
This I know
So, many changes have come and gone, but we still remain solid just holding on,
With age and maturity, our days are now claimed and bliss,
Only because we vowed to each other and sealed it with a kiss.

YOU AND ME

You loved me and I loved you,
Now I don't know if that is true,
It seems as though I'm always crying,
It seems as though you're always lying,
Where is the truth in front of my eyes,
So, you must be the one I despise,
All my trust and faith were in you,
Love was there in everything you'd do,
You changed my life, all my ideas,
And left me cold, swarming in tears,
They say don't worry cause life goes on,
I only wish that I were never born,
Not born to know life's infernal pain,
With only a loss, and never a gain.

TEARS

Just walking alone minding my business felt something queer roll down my cheek,
Had no reason no answer not even a guess,
Just one small portion made my body weak,
They came so fast and suddenly,
I asked myself what was simply wrong with me,
Tears spell jealousy, anger, and pain,
Everything was fine until they came,
They came so quick and left so slow,
Taking me back in the dreaded past; that place where I'd wish I'd never go,
For I have no feelings, no emotions at all,
So, I let my tears run and do as they pleased,
But no they just simply wish to fall.

JAMES

In the day all through the night,
I think of James, he's such a beautiful sight,
Then she came, she thought she had the right, to try to take James,
Well, I put up one hell of a fight,
I scratched her and kicked her and almost pulled her eyes out,
Fighting for my man, that's what it was all about,
She said to me, "You see your love could never be,"
She doesn't know that James wants me, or so I thought,
And to my surprise, I was taught,
I thought I was his lover,
Until I saw him with another.

LOVE

To love someone with all your heart and soul,
And give them all the time within the day,
To let them know they have a heart of gold,
To let them know that love is here to stay,
You have the love within my heart and the kind of love
that will never cease,
That's how I know we'll never part, nor lose the thrill
that comes when I see you and you see me,
If something shall ever come between us two, then I
assure you there will be a price to pay,
Only our love keeps my blood flowing, my heart
pumping each and every single day.

LOVE IS

Love is me loving you,
Love is everything you do,
Love is showing that love,
Love is the one you're thinking of,
It's so hard to express myself,
These feelings I have for no one else,
Love is having to let go,
Love is never saying no,
Love is something I wish I could steal,
Love is here in full bloom,
Love has entered and filled the room.

MEN IN MY LIFE

Men in my life are doing me wrong,
They're doing me wrong by leaving me alone,
Yes, they say I'm fine and cute,
But they leave me and they'll leave you too,
I just wish for once we could control those brutes,
They use you and abuse you and see you with someone
else and accuse you,
Well, I'm tired of hand me downs and scraps,
Someday I'll have someone worthwhile perhaps.

DON'T TAKE IT HARD

Don't take it hard, That I broke your heart,
Just wanted you to see, What you did to me,
I know it hurts, Being treated like dirt,
This is not revenge, But this shit's got to end,
So here's some advice, You better be nice,
I'm not your Barbie doll, Or just your average booty call,
I demand some respect, I won't settle for less,
For I've been told baby you're the best
And if you don't believe me,
Just put me to the test.

SWEPT AWAY

I was swept away, swept away, by his charm and grace,
And that bashful smile that brought warmth to the place,
I was swept away, swept away, but the way he entered the room,
Wishing he would be mind and very soon,
I was swept away, swept away, because he looked so fine, no plain, not simple, not the average kind,
I was swept away, swept away, his eyes so bright, those beautiful sparkling eyes that could light up a dark, misty night,
Once I saw him there came a thrill inside,
It was a loving feeling I couldn't describe,
So, believe in your fantasy without a doubt,
Because they came come true, that's what they're all about.

CONSCIOUS

Stuck between right and wrong,
Having to choose one or the other,
There's an angel inside and a devil too,
So, who's to say which will take control of you,
Controversy, conflict, and power over power, soon
you've chosen one for another,
We have a reminder to keep us in line,
Conscious I say, so bear this in mind,
With every breath you take, with every step you make,
Just remember he's there, don't make a mistake,
Temptation tastes deliciously right,
So don't let the devil win, put up a good fight.

TOO GOOD TO BE TRUE

Finding someone like you is too good to be true,
Someone that loves me and holds me and kisses all
over me,
And that's just the way a man ought to be,
Someone to give me diamonds and pearls and a
wedding ring, too,
But, I still say, it's too good to be true,
Someone that will never cheat,
Now you know that can't be beat,
Where did I find a guy like you,
And I didn't have to use voodoo,
I still say, it's too good to be true
It was just a dream… I mean,
I knew, it was too good to be true.

YOU HAVE AN UNBREAKABLE CHAIN TO MY HEART

The days and nights are very long,
Pleading for your strong yet gentle arms,
Promises are made upon love's passion, laughter, and pleasure untold,
Never to be made true, because of the forbidden love I stole,
Yet, searching my heart from one end to the next,
It will lead right back to the place where our love first met,
In the end when the body is decrepit and old,
A young girl at heart, story of love's passion will be reverently told,
My darling, I once and always will have love in my heart for you,
It will forever bind us in whatever we do.

NO FRIEND OF MINE

In the beginning, I was there for you as your friend,
But, now you're no friend of mine,
I gave to you all I had, my mind, body, and soul,
But in the end it was my heart you stole,
You took my heart and crushed it in two—Yes I don't mean anyone else but you,
You said we would be together until the end,
Like a fool I believed you and stayed your friend,
I was happy with just a little love,
I didn't need it all,
Now, these days you won't even call,
But now you've proven to be no friend of mine,
You used me for the last time,
You had your cake and ate it too,
Now you're full of me and telling me you're through,
I gave you my all as an undying friend would do,
Now when I call you won't answer,
You acted as though you loved me so,
Why you changed I may never know,
You say you're old, this relationship has gone on for too long,
Now I must brace myself and be happy and strong,
Tell myself that life goes on,
We had a bond from a twine of love and life's sacrifice,
Only if I had listened to some friends' advice,
No you are no friend of mine
For I still have care, and was devoted to the end,
But you turn your back on me now
That's No Friend!

THE NEW PLAYERS

This is to the players and no one else,
There's nothing to playing so watch yourself,
Haven't you hear, did you get the message,
Well, listen good and you'll learn your lesson,
You're called no good players and a devil in disguise,
Take it from me, that's not nice,
Forget about playing and hang up your dice,
Don't be greedy with two or three,
There's nothing wrong with just you and me,
This is to the players and all their schemes,
There's nothing to playing, it's an endless dream,
Be cool not a fool and watch yourself,
Because in the end, it could mean your death.

A HEAVY HEART

In so very many ways, love is hard to bear,
When someone special aimlessly forgets to care,
The heart gets heavy, it can feel the sharp blades that
thrust upon it like a knife,
When all your time and effort vanishes, leaving you
with an empty life,
Coming together, compromise, prayer, and holding
each other tight,
They all are ingredients to making a relationship right,
But when our love fails and is not destined to grow,
Please don't forget what brought us together
"Friendship,"
Let it shine—
Let it grow—

SECOND CHANCE

You saved me, I was lost in life,
You saved me, rescued me from my desperation,
Now I have hope, a second chance inspiration,
You saved me, My hero, My king,
For, I was indulged in an unspeakable thing,
Living my life as if it had no value at all,
Then there you appeared so valiant and tall,
You made my body rise and come alive,
With a kiss of your lips, I was then mesmerized,
You saved me, I was lost in life,
Yet you picked me up, and took me in,
Rescued me, for I was engaged in a pool of sin,
I admire your confidence, compassion, and caring,
Oh, how you've enlightened me to new experiences
that's exciting and daring,
I must thank you and bow at your feet,
For you have made my life worth living and totally
complete.

WHY YOU WISH TO BREAK MY HEART

Why you wish to break my heart,
We were together, but now we're apart,
Why you wish to break my heart,
Remember when you kissed my lips and gently touched my face,
But now I feel so out of place,
Listen to me and listen good,
I love you more than anyone else ever could,
You were my light that shined at night,
You controlled my mind, my body, my emotions,
You became my love potion,
You took my love and stumped it to the ground,
But, did I say one word or make a sound,
It's cruel, immoral and ruthless of you, to tell me to go find somebody new,
You were it, all I had….
What once was sweet…ended so sad.

UNTIL YOU CAME

My love, Love of my life,
I had to encounter so much heartache and strife,
Where were you when I needed you most, someone I search for from coast to coast,
From you I found true love, so defined and pristine just like a pure dove,
From you came the greatest of joy and deepest of pain,
Given the choice to make a change,
I would change nothing, everything would remain the same,
There would arise a time that tested our faith,
Only to prove we were the perfect mates,
We have grown like a seed planted in the ground,
Our dedication and willingness showed solid and sound,
We fit together like a glove and hand,
That makes me so assured I've found the right man.

THE KEY TO PEACE

There was silence all around,
A dry yet muffled sound,
I was torn between emotions of love, emptiness, hope, and pain,
All of which made up the ingredients of my life with little to gain,
There as I sat wondering what is the key to my happiness, my key to success,
It was merely to overcome life's turbulent test,
Joy can be found where money does not reside,
Such as, caring for a loved one at a hospital bedside,
Joy can eliminate some pain, agony, and strife,
Joy can be found in the nature of life,
Take a stroll in the park,
Take a look a beautiful scenery now that's a good start,
Taking time with a child to play and have fun,
Or awake early one morning to watch the rising sun.

ABOUT THE AUTHOR

Lisa Boyd was born on September 19, 1965 in Memphis, TN. She is the mother of a son who is soon to graduate from high school and has loved writing since she was a little girl.

When problems would arise or when something made her happy, she would put it all on paper as that was always a comfort to her, filling her with joy.

Now retired, she is living her dream of walking and jogging in the park, taking spin and boot camp classes, and yoga every week.

Boyd is current on the journey of living with stage 4 rectal cancer and is grateful for every day God gives her, believing that this book is a part of her journey to serve God's purpose.

www.ingramcontent.com/pod-product-compliance
Lightning Source LLC
Chambersburg PA
CBHW041306110426
42743CB00037B/11